SOLAR SYSTEM

Design	Cooper · West
Editor	Denny Robson
Researcher	Cecilia Weston-Baker
Illustrator	Louise Nevett
Consultant	J. W. Warren Ph.D. Formerly Reader in Physics Education, Department of Physics, Brunel University, London, UK.

SOLAR SYSTEM

Kathryn Whyman

PRICE STERN SLOAN

Los Angeles

INTRODUCTION

Look at the sky on a clear night and you can see thousands of stars. The universe contains millions more stars which are too far away to see. Our own small part of this vast universe is called the Solar System. If we could travel from one side of the Solar System to the other it would take many years.

Not surprisingly, it has been difficult for scientists to find out about the Solar System. But in this book you will begin to understand something about it. You will find out about the Sun, the moons and conditions on the planets. You will learn how people have studied and are *still* studying the Solar System and where they think it came from.

CONTENTS

WHAT IS THE SOLAR SYSTEM?

The Solar System is made up of the Sun, nine planets, several moons (the number changes as more are discovered) and a band of rocks called the Asteroid Belt. The planets and the Asteroid Belt all travel around the Sun. We say they orbit the Sun. They each take a certain time to go around the Sun. This time is the planet's year. As the planets orbit, they spin like tops. They all spin at different speeds. The time they take to spin around once is called a day. Many of the planets have moons. While the planets orbit the Sun, the moons orbit the planets.

You can see from the diagram that all the planets are different sizes. The Sun is so big compared to the planets that only a tiny part of it fits on the page!

As you can see from this table, the planets vary greatly in size and all are a very long way from the Sun. The planets closest to the Sun have the shortest years as they do not have so far to travel and they travel faster. The planets with the shortest days are the ones which spin around the fastest.

Planet	Distance from Sun (millions of miles)	Diameter (miles)	Day length (in Earth days/ hours)	Year length (in Earth days/ years)
Mercury	36	3,014	59 days	88 days
Venus	67	7,545	243 days	225 days
Earth	93	7,927	24 hours	365 days
Mars	142	4,220	24½ hours	687 days
Jupiter	484	88,630	10 hours	12 years
Saturn	887	74,700	10¼ hours	29½ years
Uranus	1,783	30,500	15½ hours	84 years
Neptune	2,795	33,000	16 hours	165 years
Pluto	3,667	1,500	6 days 9 hours	248 years

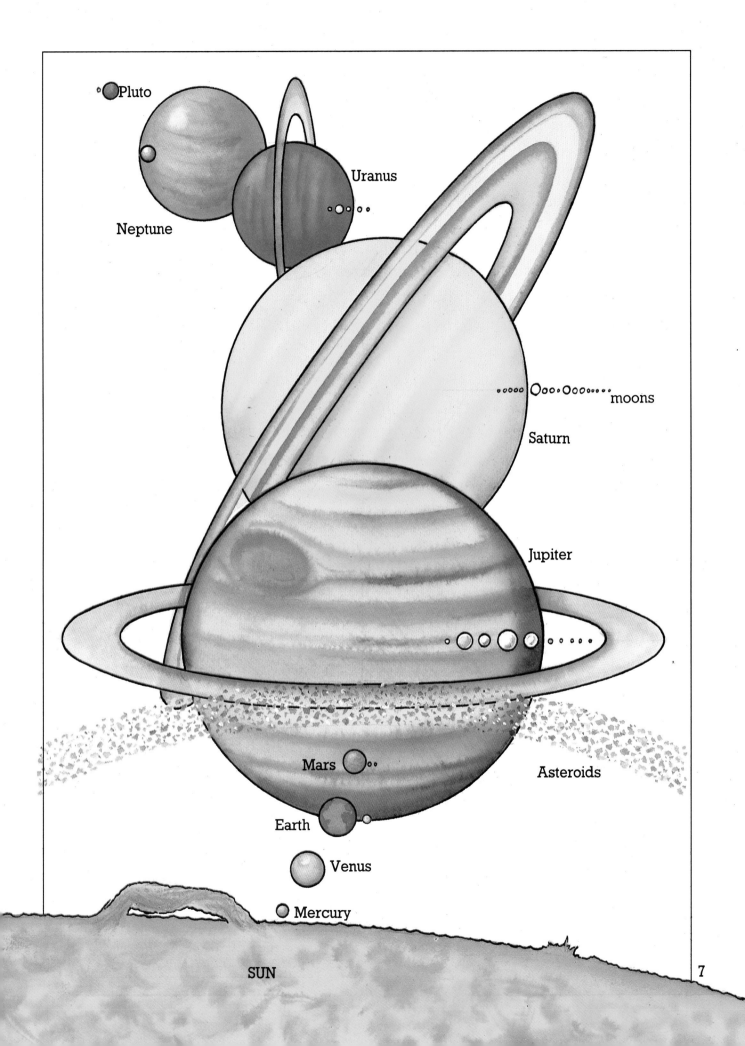

Pluto

Neptune

Uranus

moons

Saturn

Jupiter

Mars

Asteroids

Earth

Venus

Mercury

SUN

7

ORIGINS OF THE SOLAR SYSTEM

Where did the Solar System come from? Scientists think that the Sun and planets grew out of a cloud of dust and gas about 4.6 billion years ago. Part of this cloud collapsed and shrank and got very hot. This was the beginning of the Sun. The planets formed from the leftover gas and dust which circled the Sun.

Our Sun is a star. Stars form in enormous groups called galaxies. Our Sun is part of the Milky Way galaxy. Stars are so far apart that we use special units called light-years to measure the distances between them. Light travels faster than anything else in the universe. But light takes about 80,000 years to cross from one side of the Milky Way to the other! We say the Milky Way measures 80,000 light-years across.

These diagrams show how the Solar System probably began. The Sun formed first at the center of the cloud (1-3). Specks of material bumped into each other and gradually built up into lumps (4). These grew to form the planets (5).

Close to the Sun, where it was hottest, rocky planets grew which had iron at their centers. These are the inner planets. Farther from the Sun, where it was cooler, giant gas planets grew. All the planets moved around the Sun.

1

2
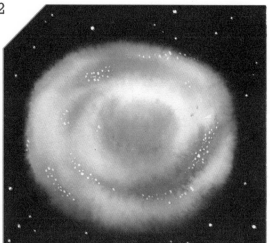

3
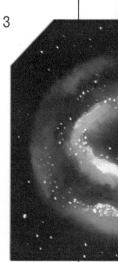

The Andromeda Galaxy, pictured here, looks much like our own galaxy

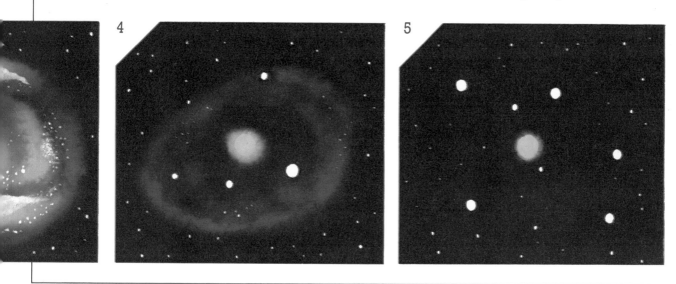

THE SUN

The Sun is the most important part of the Solar System. It keeps the planets in their orbits. Like other stars, the Sun emits radiation in the form of heat, part of which is visible as light. Energy from the Sun is essential for life on Earth.

The Sun is huge. A hollow ball the size of the Sun could hold about a million Earths! It is also extremely hot. The "surface" of the Sun reaches about 6,000°C (11,000°F). The center of the Sun is probably about 13 million degrees centigrade!

The Sun is made mostly of the gases hydrogen and helium. At its center, hydrogen is constantly being turned into helium. This is a nuclear reaction which releases huge amounts of energy. This energy travels to the surface of the Sun and then into space as radiation.

The surface of the Sun is called the photosphere. Here there are often dark patches called sunspots. These are areas of gas which are cooler than the rest of the surface. Although we call them spots, they are many times larger than the Earth. Giant jets of gas shoot out from the Sun. They are called flares. Sometimes arches of gas loop across the surface. These are known as prominences.

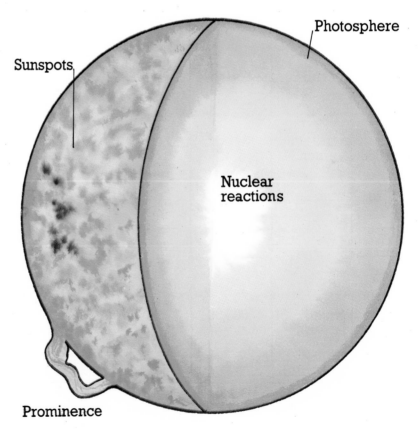

Sunspots

Photosphere

Nuclear reactions

Prominence

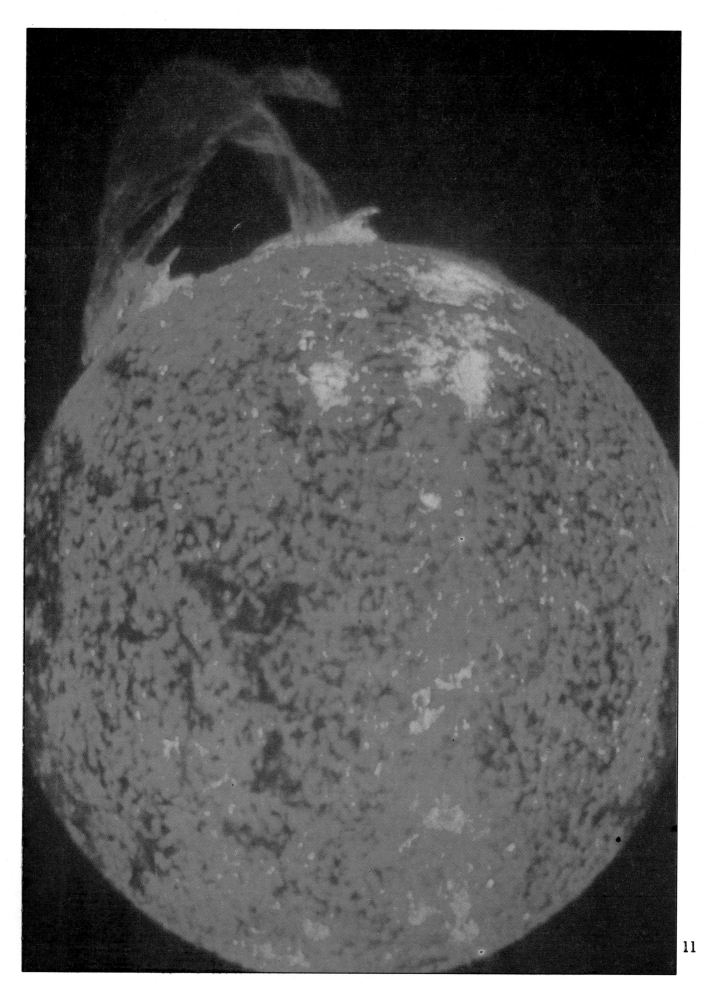

This picture of the Sun shows a giant loop prominence

THE INNER PLANETS

The inner planets – Mercury, Venus, Earth and Mars – are all made of rock. They are quite small compared with some of the other planets. Mercury is closest to the Sun. It is extremely hot during the day but the temperature falls to −175°C (−283°F) at night. Mercury is only a little bigger than our Moon.

Although Venus is farther from the Sun than Mercury, it is the hottest planet in the Solar System. Venus spins in the opposite direction to all the other planets. It also spins very slowly – so slowly that its "day" is longer than its "year"!

Earth has water, oxygen and moderate temperatures. Because of this it can support life. Mars has about half the diameter of Earth. Temperatures here are seldom above 0°C (32°F) and the only water is the ice in the planet's soil.

An impression of the spacecraft Venera on the surface of Venus

MERCURY	VENUS	EARTH	MARS
Like the Moon, the surface of Mercury is pitted with craters and covered in dust and stones. There is no air or water. It is bathed in dangerous radiation from the Sun.	On the surface of Venus there are deep cracks and dead volcanoes. The atmosphere is thick carbon dioxide gas and the planet is surrounded by clouds of sulfuric acid.	About three quarters of the Earth's surface is covered by water. The atmosphere contains the gases oxygen, nitrogen and a small amount of carbon dioxide.	Mars is made of red rocks. There are craters and dead volcanoes. The atmosphere is dusty and made of carbon dioxide. There are strong winds which blow up dust storms.

THE GIANT PLANETS

Jupiter and Saturn are the two largest and fastest spinning planets in the Solar System. They are both made mostly of the gases hydrogen and helium. Jupiter is the largest. It weighs two and a half times as much as all the other planets put together. Its outer layer of gas clouds is about 1,000 km (620 miles) thick. Fierce winds blow these clouds and huge streaks of lightning flash between them. Below the cloud layer the gases get denser and denser until they become liquid.

Saturn is made of less dense gases. In fact Saturn could float on water! The planet looks very beautiful because it is surrounded by rings. The rings are not solid. They are made of pieces of rock and ice and snow which orbit the planet.

Here we see Jupiter with its volcanic moon Io in the foreground

This picture is made up of photographs of Saturn and several of its moons

THE OUTER PLANETS

Uranus, Neptune and Pluto are the planets farthest from the Sun. They get very little of the Sun's radiation so they are all dark and cold places. Uranus and Neptune are large planets made of gas. They look greenish-blue because they contain a gas called methane. Uranus is circled by nine rings, which are smaller than the rings around Saturn. The rings seem to be made of rocks and ice.

Pluto is the greatest mystery of all. It was only discovered in 1930 and is even smaller than our Moon. It is probably made of rock and covered in ice. Pluto is usually the outermost planet. But sometimes it comes nearer to the Sun than Neptune for about 20 years, and then Neptune is the outermost planet. This happened last in 1979.

Voyager 2's view of Uranus after its closest approach to the planet

This artwork shows the Voyager 2 space probe as it passes Neptune's north pole

An artist's impression of the planet Pluto and its moon Charon

THE MOONS

A moon is a ball of rock which orbits a planet. Mercury and Venus are the only planets which do not have moons. Jupiter and Saturn each have at least 16 moons. Our Moon is our closest neighbor in space. Moons may be lumps of material which were left over when the planets formed. Like planets, moons can only be seen when they are lit up by the Sun.

Our Moon takes 27 ½ days to orbit the Earth. During this time it seems to change shape. This is because only the side of the Moon which faces the Sun is lit up. And as the Moon orbits the Earth we see different amounts of this lit-up side.

When the Moon is between the Sun and the Earth we cannot see it. This is called a New Moon. A Full Moon is when the Earth is between the Sun and the Moon. The diagrams show phases of the Moon seen in the Northern Hemisphere.

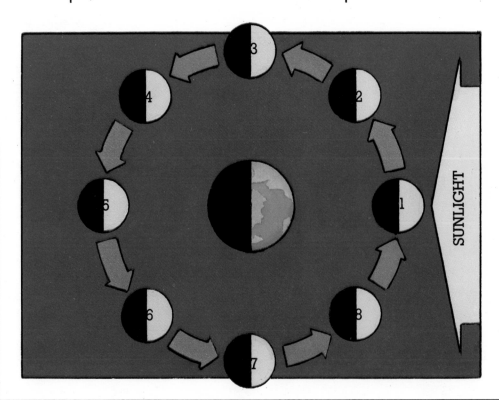

SUNLIGHT

1 New

2 Crescent

3 1st Quarter

4 Gibbous

5 Full

6 Gibbous

7 Last Quarter

8 Crescent

We know more about our own Moon than any other member of the Solar System, apart from the Earth. Astronauts have even landed on the Moon. The Moon is a bare, dead place where nothing lives or grows. Its surface has hills and mountains as well as flat plains and deep craters. There is no water or air on the Moon and it is covered with a layer of fine dust. From the Moon, the sky always looks black and the Earth seems to change shape and go through phases.

Seen from the Moon (foreground), the Earth appears to change shape

FORCES IN THE SOLAR SYSTEM

The planets travel around the Sun in nearly circular paths. This means they are constantly changing direction. There must be a force which makes the planets turn. This force is called gravity. You can feel the force of the Earth's gravity – without it you would float up into space! Gravity is a force which pulls. All the planets exert gravity. The more massive they are, the stronger is their pull of gravity. The Sun is so massive that its gravity is strong enough to keep all the planets turning around it. Without this force, they would each fly off in a straight line.

The Moon also has gravity. Because it is less massive than the Earth, its pull of gravity is weaker – as this astronaut found out!

Like the planets, this ball will keep moving in a circle as long as it travels fast enough. The force which acts along the string pulls the ball and makes it change direction. Although a different kind of force, its effect can be compared to the gravity exerted by the Sun. If the child let go of the string, there would be no pulling force to keep the ball turning. It would fly away in a straight line.

Pluto

Neptune

Uranus

An astronaut leaps from the Moon's surface while saluting the US flag

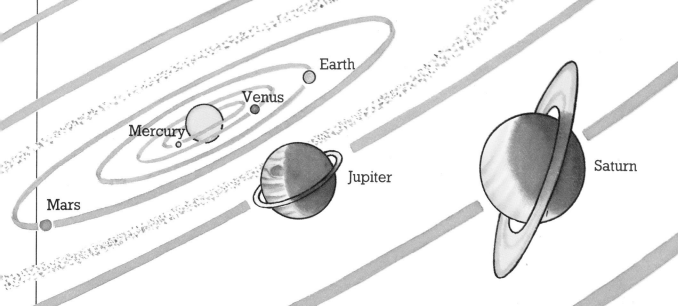

Earth

Venus

Mercury

Jupiter

Saturn

Mars

VISITORS TO THE SOLAR SYSTEM

Occasionally we see comets in our Solar System. A comet has a nucleus which is a ball made of ice and rock. This is surrounded by a cloud of gas called the coma. When comets move close enough to the Sun, they reflect the Sun's light and form a tail of gas and dust.

Comets leave bits of dust from their tails behind in space. Some of this dust enters the Earth's atmosphere where it burns up. We may then see a shower of bright shooting stars. The scientific name for a shooting star is a meteor.

Sometimes lumps of rock or metal from space crash to the Earth. They are meteorites. A large meteorite may make a hole where it lands called a crater. Meteorites caused the craters on the surface of the Moon, Mercury and Mars – as well as this one in Arizona.

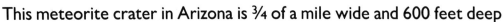

This meteorite crater in Arizona is ¾ of a mile wide and 600 feet deep

HALLEY'S COMET

Halley's comet is a regular visitor to our part of the Solar System. It returns about every 76 years, and has been seen throughout the ages. The diagram shows the strange shape of the comet's orbit – a long oval. The comet is invisible beyond Saturn's orbit. You can see how the comet's tail always points away from the Sun.

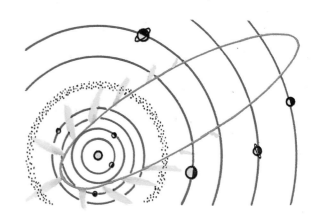

An artist's impression of the space probe *Giotto* monitoring the comet's visit in 1986

OBSERVING THE SOLAR SYSTEM

People have always watched the planets and stars. But they are too far away to see clearly, however good your eyesight is. The telescope was invented to help people look at faint, distant objects and see them in more detail. Telescopes collect more light than the human eye. They also make things look bigger. Stars and planets looked at through a telescope seem to be brighter and closer.

Telescopes use either a lens or a mirror to collect light and focus it. Another lens is used to produce a magnified image. Modern telescopes are housed in giant buildings called observatories. These are often built at the top of a high mountain where there is a clear view of the sky. Astronomers watch the movements of the stars and planets through telescopes.

This telescope uses one convex lens to collect and focus light, and another to magnify the image. Sliding the outer tube changes the distance between the two lenses. This is important as it allows near and far objects to be seen clearly.

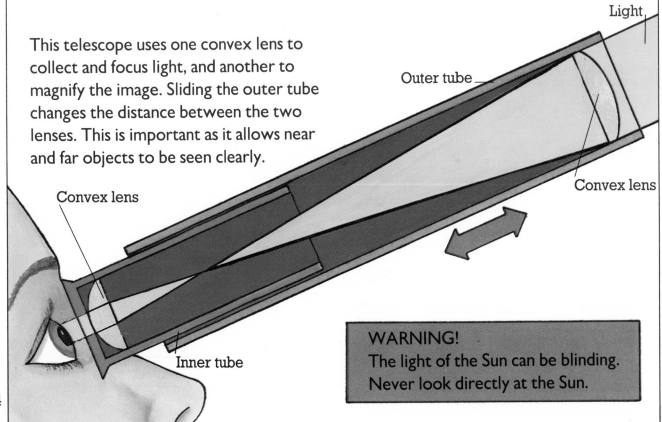

Light

Outer tube

Convex lens

Convex lens

Inner tube

WARNING!
The light of the Sun can be blinding. Never look directly at the Sun.

Looking down on a telescope in the observatory at Kitt Peak, Arizona

Watching the Solar System from the Earth is one way of finding out about it. To learn more, people have used rockets to travel into space. There they have been able to look at parts of the Solar System more clearly. But although the first men landed on the Moon in 1969, no one has visited any of the planets. They are too far away and conditions are too dangerous for humans.

However, as you have seen from the pictures in this book, space probes – robot-controlled unmanned spacecraft – have been sent far into the Solar System. The space probe Voyager 2 is on a journey to the edge of the Solar System. As it travels it takes pictures of the planets and sends them back to Earth. Voyager 2 is expected to reach Neptune in 1989.

This is a diagram of Voyager 2. This space probe has already traveled across millions of miles of space, and has collected information on Jupiter, Saturn and Uranus. The craft's onboard computers are reprogrammed during its flight by electronic signals from Earth. The entire vehicle weighs only 1,800 lbs. It carries equipment for 11 scientific experiments which are powered by a nuclear generator.

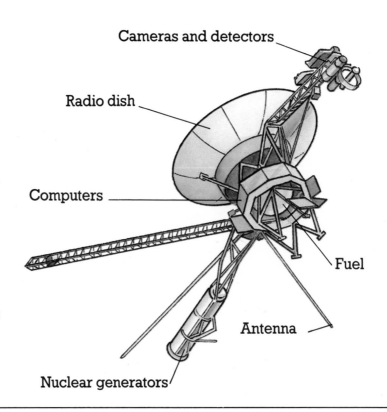

Cameras and detectors

Radio dish

Computers

Fuel

Antenna

Nuclear generators

This is an *actual* photograph of the surface of Mars taken by Viking 2 lander

MAKE YOUR OWN MOBILE

You can have the Solar System hanging from your ceiling! This mobile is easy to make. It will help you remember some of the things you have learned about the Solar System.

Trace the shapes of the members of the Solar System onto cardboard and cut them out. Fit rings around Saturn, Jupiter and Uranus. Use the diagram below to measure lengths of strong string. Remember to cut them longer so you have enough to fix the ends. Fix each piece of string to the top of its planet. Hang the planets from the Sun and color them, as shown in the diagram. Attach string to either end of the Sun and your mobile is now ready to hang.

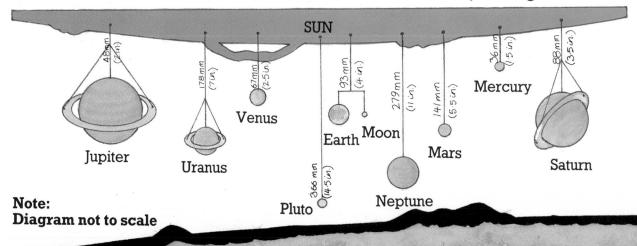

Note:
Diagram not to scale

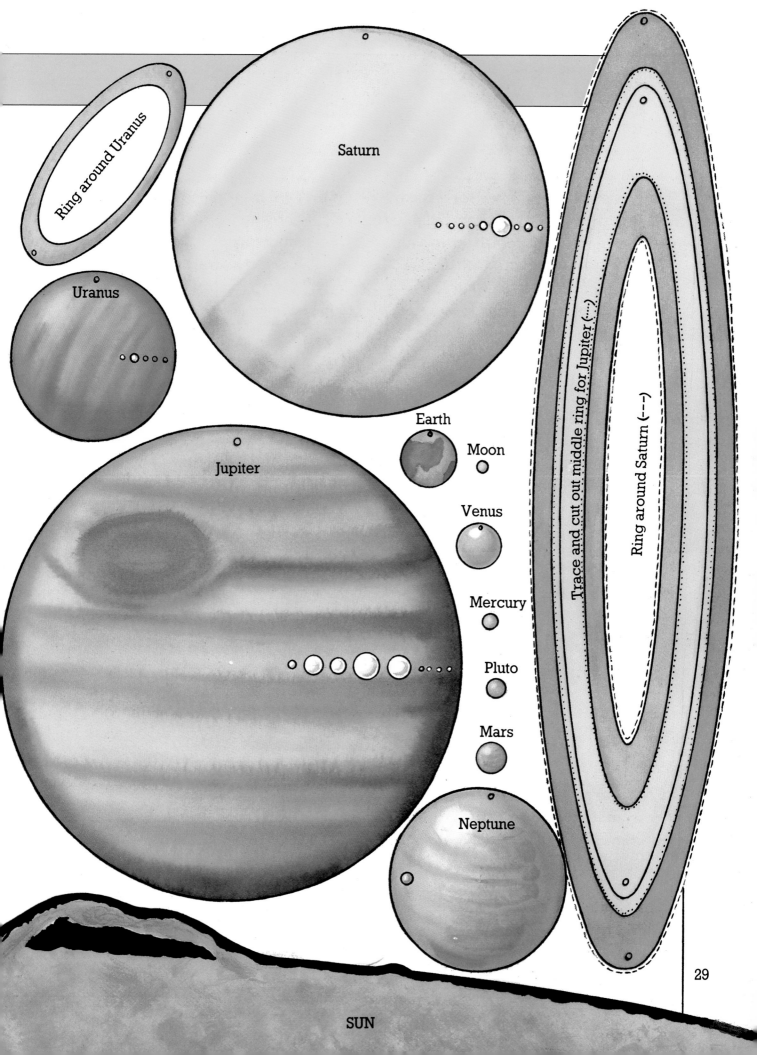

Ring around Uranus

Saturn

Uranus

Earth

Moon

Venus

Jupiter

Mercury

Pluto

Mars

Neptune

Trace and cut out middle ring for Jupiter (·····)

Ring around Saturn (– – –)

SUN

Life and death of a star

When a star like our Sun first forms it is different from the way we see it today. At first the Sun was a very hot, blue star. As it grew bigger it cooled down and looked white. The Sun will shine as a white star for about 10 billion years. Eventually it will swell and form a Red Giant. Some of the stars we see are Red Giants. They are cooler than the Sun. But as they are many times bigger, they appear brighter. A Red Giant slowly cools and shrinks. Its outer layers of gas drift away and a small hot star called a White Dwarf is left. This slowly cools and becomes a Black Dwarf.

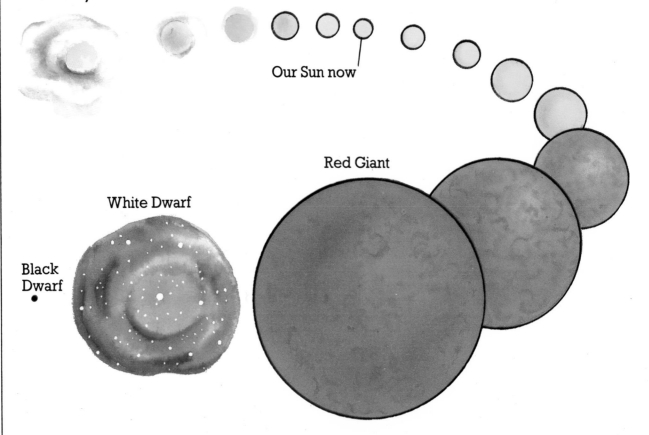

Our Sun now

Red Giant

White Dwarf

Black Dwarf

Very large stars

Stars much bigger than our Sun also become Red Giants, but they blow up in a huge explosion called a supernova. They shrink into themselves and form a Black Hole. Anything nearby gets sucked into a black hole. In February 1987, the brightest super nova since 1604 appeared in the skies.

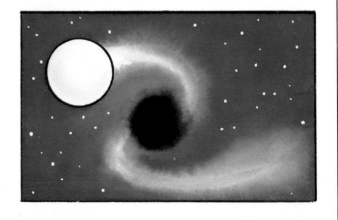

GLOSSARY

Asteroid
A piece of rock floating in space. The Asteroid Belt is a band of thousands of asteroids between Mars and Jupiter.

Astronaut
Someone who travels in space.

Astronomer
A scientist who studies the stars, planets and galaxies.

Atmosphere
A thin blanket of gases which surrounds a planet. The gases are held in place by the gravity of the planet.

Convex lens
A piece of glass which is thicker in the middle than at the edges. Light is brought to a focus after passing through a convex lens.

Galaxy
A group of millions of stars. Galaxies can be different shapes and sizes. There are millions of them in the Universe.

Image
The picture of an object which you see when you look at it through a lens or in a mirror.

Light-year
This is a unit of distance. It is the distance that light travels in one Earth year. It is equal to approx. 6 trillion miles.

Magnify
Make something look bigger than it really is.

Moon
A ball of rock which orbits around a planet.

Planet
A big ball of substances (such as rocks, liquids and gases) which orbits the Sun.

Radiation
Movement of light, and other rays, from hot bodies such as the Sun through space to the planets.

Rocket
A very powerful engine which can be used to lift spacecraft and satellites into space.

Space probes
Unmanned spacecraft sent to study other planets.

Star
A gigantic ball of very hot gases which glows. The Sun is a star.

Universe
Everything which exists, including the Solar System, our galaxy (the Milky Way) and all the other millions of galaxies. Scientists think the Universe is getting larger all the time.

INDEX

Photographic Credits:
Cover and page 9: Aspect; contents
page, title page and pages 12, 14 and 17:
David Hardy/Astro Art; pages 11, 15, 16,
17, 21 and 22: Science Photo Library;
page 25: Colorific.